D0612974

EVITA

THE LIFE & TIMES OF

Evita

BY
Amy Dempsey

||| •PARRAGON• |||

This edition first published by
Parragon Book Service Ltd in 1996

Parragon Book Service Ltd
Unit 13–17 Avonbridge Trading Estate
Atlantic Road, Avonmouth
Bristol BS11 9QD

Produced by Magpie Books,
an imprint of Robinson Publishing

Copyright © Parragon Book Service Ltd 1996

Illustrations courtesy of: Hulton Deutsch;
Peter Newark's Pictures

All rights reserved. This book is sold subject to the
condition that it shall not, by way of trade or otherwise,
be lent, resold, hired out or otherwise circulated
without the publisher's prior consent in any form of
binding or cover other than that in which it is published
and without similar condition being imposed on
the subsequent purchaser.

ISBN 0 75251 775 9

A copy of the British Library Cataloguing in Publication
Data is available from the British Library.

Typeset by Whitelaw & Palmer Ltd, Glasgow
Printed in Singapore

FROM PEASANT GIRL TO CELEBRITY

On 7 May 1919, a daughter was born to Juana Ibarguren and Juan Duarte in Los Toldos, a small village settlement in the Argentine pampa, the vast, flat, agriculturally rich plains. Named María Eva Duarte, she was the fifth child of this second, illegitimate family of Duarte's. Juana was a proud, stubborn woman who did not act like a mistress and she and the children used Duarte's name, although their legal name was Ibarguren. Duarte was a small landowner and this second family in Los Toldos lived fairly well, but without the respect and standing of his legitimate family. This discrepancy was to have a profound effect on the woman who would become known affectionately as 'Evita' to millions – the defender of the poor and enemy of the rich, who would also spend her life hiding the infamy of her birth and fighting the hypocrisy of the landed aristocracy, while simultaneously craving their approval.

Shortly after Eva's birth, Juan returned to his legitimate family in Chivilcoy and Juana began sewing clothes for people of the village in order to support the family. The villagers gossiped about her and called her names in front of the children. When Juan Duarte died in January 1926, Juana was determined that she and the children, Blanca, Elisa, Juan, Erminda, and María Eva would attend the funeral. This caused a scandal in Chivilcoy and only after pleading with the wife's brother were they allowed to see the body and walk with the crowd behind the hearse to the funeral. While the young Evita did not have many memories of her father, she was deeply affected and confused by the hate directed at her family.

In 1930 Juana moved the family to Junin where Elisa had a job in the post office. Juana called herself 'the widow Duarte' and as there were no restaurants in the town, she began to cook for the town's respectable bachelors, whom she referred to as 'guests'. While Juana presented the family as gentility fallen on hard times, her reputation suffered from this arrangement and some of the girls at Eva's school were forbidden to speak to her because of what their parents thought her mother was. Eva attended primary school in Junin, which was to be the extent of her formal education. By the age of fifteen, Eva was determined to have a different life from her mother's and she aimed to get to the bright lights of Buenos Aires to become an actress. Eva and her sisters and friends were enraptured by the images of life that Hollywood films portrayed – love, money, and beautiful clothes in sumptuous surroundings. They collected and exchanged photographs of their favourite stars from *Sintonía*, the Argentine movie tabloid, and dreamed of life in the big cities where everyone was rich and beautiful. In the 1930s, Buenos Aires was a cosmopolitan, international, cultural capital, where the rich were very rich and the poor incredibly poor. The young Eva was going there to make her fortune by whatever means necessary.

Her opportunity arrived in the form of a tango singer performing in Junin as part of a tour. She had an affair with him and persuaded him to take her to Buenos Aires – Eva was on her way. Armed with ambition, passion and determination, which were to become her trademarks, she set about making it to the top. Her detractors claim she was a prostitute in Buenos Aires at this time, but are unable to prove it. Although the label is too clear-cut, and harsh, Eva certainly knew, or learned quickly the ways of the world and show business, and most realistically did have to sleep her way up the ladder. One of her first jobs was playing a nurse in *The Fatal Kiss*, a production about the evils of social diseases, which toured Argentina. After a couple of years of bit parts, Eva began to learn the ropes. She learned the value of publicity and hung around the offices of *Sintonía*, in order to get her name in the gossip columns linked with various personalities. Whatever the methods she employed to break into the business, by 1940 she was an established actress, making her name in radio soap operas. By 1943, she was well-known and one of the best-paid radio actresses of that time.

Eva Duarte as a young actress

In June of 1943, the military took over the running of the government in Argentina, ending what was called the 'Infamous Decade' of the thirties, which was characterized by a series of fraudulent elections which kept the Oligarchy in power. Their main interest had been the concerns of the landed classes and their dealings with the British. The vague aim of the new government was to modernize the country and regulate its industries, including the radio. Eva took a proposal for a series called *Heroines of History*, which was to deal with high moral and historical themes, to the officer in charge of allocating air-time, Colonel Anibal Imbert. His assistant, Oscar Nicolini, who was to become a long-time friend of Evita's, helped get the project approved.

Evita's next big opportunity presented itself at a large fund-raiser in Buenos Aires to help the victims of an earthquake in San Juan, at which Colonel Juan Domingo Perón, Secretary of War and Labour, was the guest of honour. When the person sitting next to him left for a moment, she saw her chance and grabbed it. She slipped in next to him and remained by the captivated Perón for the rest of the show, and her life. Perón's current mistress was a young girl whom he called his daughter at public functions. Evita took care of the unpleasant details for Perón by going to his apartment one day while he was at work and packing up the girl and her belongings and sending her back home. By the time he came back from work Evita was all settled in. Within the week they appeared together in a photograph in a movie magazine, a public statement of their relationship, which was not to be hidden.

Perón was a 48-year-old widower, who looked much younger with his tall, muscular build and movie-star smile. He photographed well, had a direct and friendly manner and was the only governmental person to emerge as a figure of public interest. Whereas the rest of the soldier-bureaucrats avoided the press and the public, Perón courted both and enjoyed talking and explaining his ideas to others. As Evita captivated him, he captivated the Argentines.

While in the Secretariat of Labour, Perón initiated many changes for the betterment of the workers. Instead of ignoring or repressing the unions, he met with labour leaders to discuss their complaints, and helped to establish new unions and set up work tribunals to settle disputes internally instead of by the police. Retirement pay was set up in unionized industries and the Statute of the Peon, signed in November 1944, granted a minimum wage, paid holidays and medical care to agricultural workers. He addressed the needs of the new urban workforce that had grown up in Buenos Aires, and it is this group that became the first and most dedicated Perónists.

Eva Perón

FROM ACTRESS TO FIRST LADY

Meanwhile, Eva continued her radio work on famous heroines and was chosen to appear in an upcoming film, as she was able to obtain film stock through her connections. It was for this film, *La Cabalgata del Circo*, that Evita first bleached her hair to become the blonde that she would remain. An actors' union was formed and Evita was elected President.

Evita added a new radio programme, *Towards a Better Future*, in which she spoke about government policies, in plain language, as one woman wanting others to share her views about Perón. These programmes reached a whole new audience of potential supporters that traditional political propaganda could not – those unable to read.

While enjoying her new-found fame and wealth, she was not destined to be an empty-headed decoration. Perón's apartments were attached to his offices and Eva watched, served coffee, listened, and learned. She absorbed his ideas and became his most ardent supporter. She learned that he expected unconditional loyalty, which she was only too happy to give. Evita's presence at Perón's meetings with top politicians was completely without precedent. Her presence as a wife would have been odd enough, but as his mistress, it was perceived as scandalous and potentially damaging to his career. Perón was apparently unconcerned about such ideas and continued to allow Eva her role as observer.

Their open, unconventional relationship led to much gossip about the couple and the rumour that Eva was a prostitute began at this time. For those who feared Perón, namely, the Argentine wealthy, it validated their contempt and explained her hold over him. There were also many show business colleagues who, disgruntled by her success, which was certainly a direct effect of her relationship with Perón, were happy to participate in the defamation of her character. Perón's supporters would often gather outside the apartment shouting, 'Get married, get married.' Even those who knew the couple found their relationship difficult to grasp and provided such fantastic notions that it was a non-sexual coupling of two souls joined by their desire for power, or that it was purely a remedy for Perón's impotence, which could only be cured by young girls.

Evita's next film, which was to be her last, was *The Prodigal,* in which she again gained her part by being able to provide the scarce film stock through Perón. It took several months to make as shooting had to fit in around her radio work and appearances at

galas and awards ceremonies. A rough cut
was finished by September 1945, but
before it could be released her life was to
have changed dramatically and her acting
career ended. In the ten years of her acting
career she appeared in 20 plays, five films
and more than 25 soap operas.

As Perón's power and popularity grew, so
too did opposition to him. The summer of
1945 saw one of numerous anti-Perón
demonstrations, and many within the army
itself were wary of his power and his
relationship with Evita, and pushed for his
resignation. This faction threatened to
storm the city if he did not, and so, to avoid
bloodshed, Perón resigned. His farewell
speech at the Labour Secretariat was
attended by 15,000 supporters whom he

encouraged to continue the struggle for peace and received an ovation. His detractors were furious and called for his arrest and internment. He was detained on the island of Martín García by the navy. His whereabouts were kept secret and the military doctor, Colonel Mazza, took news to Evita of Perón who was eventually transferred to a military hospital in Buenos Aires. Meanwhile, Perón's staff at the Secretariat of Labour were busy organizing strikes for 18 October, both on his behalf and to alert any new government to the position of Labour.

Perón's instructions to Evita were that she hide and stay out of danger until his release, at which time they would get married, whatever the future may hold. She followed his orders and hid at the house of her acting coach upon Perón's arrest, although Perónist myth has her organizing the workers' demonstration that was to follow. The workers were furious and had no intention of relinquishing the gains they had made with Perón on their side, and thousands spontaneously took to the streets on 17 October, marching on Government House and demanding his release. Faced with the presence of 200,000 supporters, Perón's captors released him, and elections were announced for 12 February 1946, with Perón as one of the candidates. He announced his resignation from the army and his desire to become one of, and to serve, his supporters – *los descamisados*, 'the shirtless ones'. The crowd cheered, roared his name and pledged their love and fraternity. Perón addressed the crowd and beseeched them to spend the next day, which had been planned as a general strike, not actively demonstrating but celebrating. As much as it was Perón's victory, it was also the victory of the masses. The working classes had entered national politics, made their mark, and could never be ignored again. They had demanded Perón's liberation and it was granted. Argentinian politics would never again be the same.

On 10 December 1945, Colonel Juan Perón quietly married Eva, making her Señora María Eva Duarte de Perón. By this time the altering of her past had begun. Her original birth certificate was destroyed and a false one created that listed her legal name as Duarte and her parents as married.

Records of her acting career were gathered – photographs, negatives, and the only copy of her last film, *The Prodigal*, which was presented as a gift to Evita.

The response to the fairy-tale marriage was deeply divided along class lines, particularly amongst women. Those of the working classes were very supportive of his having made an honest woman of her, while middle-class women were outraged that he should have married such a woman. Eva was bitterly hurt by their comments which only served to intensify her hatred of the well-off.

During the campaign, Eva stayed in the background, studying the way to address and capture a crowd and how to instill loyalty in your followers and fear in your enemies. She was the first candidate's wife to stand beside her husband during an electoral campaign and the crowds were fascinated by her. The politicization of Eva Perón had begun.

Perón was elected President and took power on 4 June 1946 with the 27-year-old Eva as his First Lady. Her first concerns were to settle old scores and to flaunt her success. She wore extravagant, opulent clothes with ever brassier blonde hair in elaborate styles. Her scorn was reserved for those in show business or society who had belittled her or had been political opponents. Many important actors and actresses found themselves blacklisted, and, unable to find work, had to leave the

Newly elected President Perón with his wife

country. The *Sociedad de Beneficiencia* was
the next to suffer. It was a charity run by
the social elite whose custom it was to
bestow the honorary presidency on the
First Lady. When no invitation had been
issued after two months, Eva pursued the
matter, to be told that she was too young
for the position. When she suggested her
mother, the committee refused and found
their society closed by the Government
almost immediately. Eva did not stop here.
Two of the wealthiest members, Mrs de
Alvear, President, and Mrs Olmos, had
built churches in Buenos Aires which
earned them each a Vatican marquisate and
special dispensation to be buried in the
churches they had donated, instead of in a
municipal cemetery. These dispensations
were revoked and they were notified that

in order to get them renewed, they would have to discuss the matter with Mrs Perón over tea. Mrs Olmos invited Mrs Perón to tea and won her over by saying, 'My child, you are so much prettier than you look in photographs.' The dispensation was renewed. Mrs de Alvear, however, did not attempt to gain Eva's approval by inviting her to tea; a decision that Eva would not overlook. Upon Mrs de Alvear's death four years later, the police were called in to reroute the burial procession from the church to the cemetery. Eva had neither forgotten nor forgiven. For the Peróns, there was no room for those who did not show unconditional loyalty or approval.

Once she had established herself at the centre of society and made clear the consequences to those who did not accept this, the new First Lady turned her energies to more worthwhile causes – those of labour and the needy. She was as passionate with her causes as she was ruthless with her enemies. Her actions were always based on emotion – be it defending those who could not help themselves or attacking those who she perceived to be attacking her, or her loved ones. In her offices at the Ministry of Labour she received delegations and individuals most of the day, so that by the end of the Peróns' first year in power, she served as an unofficial minister of health and labour providing trade unions and the poor with an ear that led straight to the President. Her devotion endeared her to the people who knew that she was one of them. As she took centre stage in

Argentina, soon too, would she make her mark on the international scene.

Evita was formally invited to visit Spain in 1947. Perón himself could not accept the invitation as it might compromise Argentina's position in the post-war atmosphere. Argentina was suffering the recriminations of having remained neutral during the Second World War and dodging accusations of fascism, so it would not do for Perón himself to be too heavily identified with Franco. It was decided that Evita could go in an unofficial capacity, bringing 'a message of peace' to Europe and promoting the 'New Argentina'. Other countries were added to the itinerary, including Italy, France, Portugal, Monaco, and Switzerland. Her friend

Liliane Guardo, who advised her on clothing and protocol, her brother Juan, her hairdresser, two journalists and a photographer were amongst those in the party. After a number of farewell receptions, on 6 June 1947 the whole Government and a large crowd of supporters saw her off. The crowd cheered as she kissed Perón goodbye and waved farewell.

Evita arrived to a tumultuous reception in Spain, with Franco and his family and cabinet to greet her, along with a crowd of 3,000,000 Spaniards lining the streets of Madrid shouting her name. On her fifteen days in Spain, she toured the cities and countryside and attended numerous banquets and festivals thrown in her

In Switzerland, 1947

honour. The next stop was Italy, where she was granted an audience with the Pope and where her presence caused a number of demonstrations by the Communist Party, which were countered by supporters chanting her name. The reaction to her visit in France was mixed, where they were not sure what to make of this small, beautiful, bejewelled woman, but Evita was delighted to discover the Paris fashion houses, particularly Christian Dior and Marcel Rochas. She was presented with the Légion d'Honneur by the French Foreign Minister and then went to Lisbon and Switzerland. The party sailed home on the *Buenos Aires*, an Argentine ship with over 300 Italian immigrants on board to whom Evita made speeches about Perónism. In Rio de Janeiro she attended the Inter-

American Conference for Peace and Security and was mobbed outside her hotel. It was then back to Buenos Aires where she was greeted by other ships blowing their sirens, a plane circling above with WELCOME painted on its wings, a large crowd, and her beloved General Perón. Evita considered the trip a success and came back with a new sense of self-worth and a sense of the importance of the position she occupied.

Eva would later distinguish between her roles as 'Eva Perón', the President's wife performing ceremonial functions, and 'Evita', the woman performing social and political work. The European tour was the height of Eva Perón, the Evita character began to take much more prominence upon her return. The development was gradual, beginning with a more restrained appearance. She began to dress in expensive, but simple tailored suits with her hair a softer shade and pulled back in the severe style that would become her trademark. For formal occasions she would still dress the part, but in a more sophisticated fashion.

EVITA

Although there were plenty of repressive acts during Perón's regime, most significantly silencing the opposition press, he did enact numerous significant social reforms. In 1947, Argentine women were given the right to vote, after fifteen similar bills had failed to pass in the previous 35 years. In 1949, Evita founded the Perónist Women's Party which, like all Perónist vehicles, pledged loyalty to Perón, and addressed the injustices of working women. It was an incredibly successful organization, with over 500,000 members in 1952. Many joined because of Evita, and they were the first Argentine women to take an active role in politics. They became a powerful block, giving Perón a large majority in the 1951 elections with over 63 per cent of the women's vote.

The style of politics of Perón and Evita was unlike anything that had gone before in Argentina. The formal banquets and meetings were replaced with appearances at football games, openings of factories, visits to hospitals, medal presentations, and ribbon-cutting ceremonies. Perón and Evita were constantly in the public eye and interacting with the public. The 'New

Patron of *Los Descamisados*

Argentina' was based on generating emotion and public affirmation. They were not interested in those who had traditionally been powerful in politics and society, the Oligarchy, but in those formerly disaffected – the workers, women, the destitute – their beloved *descamisados*. One American reporter noted in 1948 that 'In Argentina today, it's love, love, love. Love makes the Peróns go round. Their whole act is based on it. They are constantly, madly, passionately, nationally in love. They conduct their affair with the people quite openly. They are the perfect lovers – generous, kind, and forever thoughtful in matters great and small.'

By 1948 both Perón and Evita were

powerful orators and the cult of Perón
grew. Perón and his supporters had taken
to wearing informal short-sleeved shirts –
the soldier who had become one of the
workers. He did not patronize or con-
descend to his supporters but spoke to them
as equals, equals fighting for the same
ideals. Evita was one of them, a peasant girl
who had been saved by Perón, and this was
how she addressed the crowds. Her
speeches were passionate, emotional, and
often improvised, proclaiming her love for
Perón and the people, and her role as the
bridge between them. The most important
day in the Perónist calendar was 17
October, when over a million people
would fill the Plaza de Mayo. The birth of
Perónism was re-enacted, that of the
people taking the city, claiming it as their

own and demanding the release of Perón. It was a great public reaffirmation of love in which Evita now had an equal part.

The unofficial welfare work that Evita had been doing since 1946, which consisted primarily of distributing packages of food, shoes, and furniture to those who petitioned her for help, was spiralling out of control. Although receiving donations from manufacturers and money from a special fund set up by the Ministry of Finance, the number of requests far outweighed what she and Atilio Renzi, Steward of the Residence, could deliver in his pick-up truck. By May 1948 Evita was receiving over 12,000 requests each day. On 8 July 1948, the Eva Perón Foundation was formed to provide the 'basic needs for a better life of the less privileged classes', based on the judgement of its founder.

The Foundation was free from Government control and funded by private donations. It had 14,000 permanent employees, a large percentage of them construction workers, and made annual purchases of 400,000 pairs of shoes, 500,000 sewing machines, and 200,000 cooking pots for distribution. The Foundation built new schools, hospitals, and housing, provided toys for children, scholarships for higher education, and sports facilities. Whatever her people wanted, the Foundation made it possible.

When the Foundation was created Argentina was a very wealthy country, with

Eva at work, 1950

both the working and professional classes enjoying a new, higher standard of living. Individuals and companies were willing and able to support the Foundation and Evita's position made it foolish to refuse a request for gifts. The support she had shown the unions was now repaid in kind. Union donations, in either cash or goods, provided the major source of income for the Foundation. When a union negotiated a wage increase, the first two weeks of the rise would be set aside and donated to the Foundation, and by 1950, a statutory donation of two man-days' salary per worker per union was instituted. Other sources of revenue came from a proportion of each lottery ticket, cinema ticket, and horse race admission sold, and money lost at casinos. Congress also occasionally voted funds for welfare projects. Even with the large amount of money going through its hands, and Evita's lack of interest in the accounting side of the project, the institution was remarkably untainted by corruption.

Those who wanted something from Evita were encouraged to write to her with their request and then visit her in her office. Her afternoons were kept free for this 'direct help' which eventually took up most of her day, so that visiting dignitaries and union officials had to fit in with her schedule and while waiting came into direct contact with those who were the recipients of her welfare and theirs. Each supplicant was personally received by Evita who listened to their request, chatted and joked with them and sent them away with a slip of what they would receive and a 50 peso note to help them get home. The goods would be delivered by a team of social workers. While the visit to Evita was not technically necessary, it was this human contact that made the work so special. She spoke to the supplicants not as the President's wife, but as one of them, one who was no longer poor, but knew where they were coming from and was in a position to help and wanted to help. She usually gave more than they asked for and they went away feeling that the President's wife genuinely cared for their well-being.

Evita threw herself into her work with a missionary zeal and her speeches adopted an even more outraged tone in attacking social injustice and the plight of the poor. As important as the material gifts she bestowed was the way in which it was done, with the gestures of love that accompanied the donations diminishing the shame of being on the receiving end of charity. Much to the consternation of those around her, she embraced the ragged, covering herself with lice, and kissed and let herself be kissed by the leprous and the syphilitic. These Christian gestures restored the people's respect and many called her a saint.

The Foundation built twelve hospitals of the highest international standards, so that public health care would equal or surpass that of private health care for the wealthy. The main one in Buenos Aires, the

A portrait, 1950

Policlínico Presidente Perón, while serving the poor neighbourhood where it was located, also became a medical centre and teaching hospital employing the best doctors in the country. Treatment and drugs were supplied free of charge and a hospital train was sent around the country to provide X-rays, inoculations, and medicine to those who needed it.

Over 1,000 schools were built and then turned over to the State to operate. Nursing homes, shelters for single-parent families, a home for young girls coming to Buenos Aires to look for work, and the 'Children's City' were built. The 'Children's City' housed 450 of the poorest and most neglected children that the Foundation's social workers had discovered. They were clothed, educated, and taught how to care for themselves, with the aim that when they left the home and could attend school they would not fall behind.

The work of the Foundation reflected its founder: practical and personal and expensive. While there were allegations of waste from the Opposition, and the hospitals were expensive, they were top quality and lasted, and provided equal medical care for the first time in Argentina. Even when inflation rose dramatically in 1950 the Foundation continued to grow since the material gifts it received were less affected, and it continued to supply subsidised housing and food stores. Everything that went out from the

The Peróns dressed for a gala at the theatre

Foundation bore its initials, and walls of buildings were inscribed with Perón's sayings and portraits of Evita and Perón. Of even greater propaganda value for Perónism were, however, the very tangible results that the Eva Perón Foundation provided.

In January 1950 Evita fainted at a ribbon-cutting ceremony and was rushed to hospital. She had an appendectomy and Masses were said in churches all over the country for her recovery. One of the doctors examining her, Dr Oscar Ivanissevich, noticed a growth in her womb and suggested further tests and rest. She ignored his advice and worked even harder in the months following her operation.

She worked around the clock, returning home in the early hours of the morning, often with those with whom she had been working, have breakfast with them, sleep for a few hours and then go back to work. Perón and her doctor insisted that she spend long weekends at San Vicente resting. She spent most of the time on the phone and Perón had the wires cut. Evita had it reconnected and hid the instrument under a cushion so that he would not hear it ring. Her family and friends' attempts to get her to slow down or take care of herself went unheeded. Perón wrote of these years, 'In every real sense, I had lost my wife. We saw each other only occasionally and then only briefly, as if we lived in different cities. Eva would work all night for many nights and come back at dawn. I

Evita, 1951

used to leave the Residence at six in the morning to go to the Casa Rosada and I met her at the front door, exhausted but satisfied with her work.'

In 1950 Evita was approached by the journalist Manuel Penella da Silva offering to ghost-write her autobiography. The work went through many variations, variously rewritten by Penella da Silva and then one of Perón's scriptwriters, Raúl Mende. The final draft that was accepted by Perón and Evita is like a long conversation based on many of her speeches, with the focus on her love for Perón and the people. *La Razón de mi Vida* (in English, *My Mission in Life*) perpetrated the myth of Perón the good father and of Evita the ideal woman – loving, humble, and self-sacrificing.

Eva in one of her spectacular costumes

By the end of 1950, Perón's extravagant spending on social and economic policies had begun to take its toll. As the rest of the world economy slowly improved, the need for Argentina's exports lessened and inflation began to hit not only the middle classes but also the skilled labourers. Disaffection led to a railway strike that was crushed by Perón. 1951 was the year of the presidential election and Evita had been campaigning on Perón's behalf since 1948. Her own work with women, the unions, and the Foundation had brought her an avid following of unconditional supporters. Her beauty, power, and giving had raised her to the status of cult icon. Perón himself was surprised by the depth and intensity of their support as they called for Evita to run as Vice-President. Perón was aware that

The Peróns acknowledge popular support

this would be unacceptable to many
sectors, especially the army, who would
certainly not accept a woman in the role of
President or Commander-in-Chief, if he
was to die. Popular pressure for her nom-
ination continued to grow and culminated
in a big rally on 22 August 1951.

Over a million people gathered to express
their support for a Perón-Perón ticket.
Perón, his ministers and union officials
took the stage but could not begin speaking
over the cries for Evita. Evita was brought
on stage and made her most passionate
speech to date about Perón, the people and
her mission to help the poor, but made no
direct mention of her candidacy. Her
speech ended with her saying that her only
ambition was to be Evita and to help ease

suffering. The crowd took this as a refusal and a million people began to shout for her acceptance. She took the microphone and pleaded for them to understand why she was not interested in such honours, but the crowd would not relent. Finally, José Espejo, the labour leader, took the microphone and said that Evita would give her answer in two hours. The reply the crowd received was still ambiguous, 'Comrades, as General Perón has said, I will do what the people say.' The crowd was appeased and dispersed peacefully. A week later Evita made a radio broadcast to the nation announcing her 'irrevocable, and definitive decision to renounce the honour'. Evita was forced by Perón to step down, but the gesture came to be read as one of self-sacrifice, loyalty and humility.

in store for him the moment he was told, as his first wife, Aurelia, had suffered from the same illness and, after they had tried and failed with every type of treatment, she had died in great pain, which affected him more than her.' The true nature of her illness was kept from Evita and when it was finally necessary to make a public announcement, it was called 'an anaemia of great intensity'.

Groups of workers and Perónist militants began holding Masses for her health. 92 organizations held Masses for her in the first two weeks of October. On the 6th, a 'march of silence' was held by the construction industry's trucking union. More than 1000 trucks assembled and drove slowly around Palermo Park, ending the convoy by taking a bunch of flowers and a message of sympathy to the Presidential Residence.

La Razón de mi Vida was published the following week. 150,000 copies sold on the first day and over a half-million were sold during the first month, making it the best-selling book in Argentine history.

Over a million and a half people crowded into the Plaza de Mayo for the 17 October celebration of her renunciation. After a strong dose of morphine, she was able to stand on the stage to receive two medals, one from the unions for her renunciation, which 'had the greatness of the actions of saints and martyrs', and the Grand Perónist Medal, Extraordinary Grade, awarded by

Perón for the first time. Evita was over-
come by emotion and could not speak and
was carried away. Perón took the microphone and for the first time discussed his
wife's work. It was a moving tribute to her
career as link with the unions, creator of
the Foundation, and creator of the
Women's Party. Evita had never heard
such words from Perón and rose and fell
onto him, hugging and sobbing. The
crowd 'witnessed this extraordinary scene
in utter silence, a lump in its throat'. She
made her final impassioned speech, begging
the crowd to protect and support Perón, as
she was no longer able. She fell into Perón's
arms as the crowd chanted her name.

She continued to deteriorate and it was
decided that surgery could no longer be

The dying Evita with Perón after his inauguration, June 1952

delayed. Dr George Pack was flown in from New York to perform the hysterectomy to try to contain the cancer. She never regained her strength and had to remain in bed for most of the rest of her days.

Perón, meanwhile, won the election and Evita was determined to be by his side during the Inaugural Day celebrations. A steel and plastic support was constructed for her that was welded to the floor of the convertible car. It was hidden by the fur coat that she wore, which by this time was much too large for her, as her weight had dropped to less than eighty pounds. She stood next to Perón and waved and smiled at the crowd. She had needed a triple-dose of painkillers before and a double dose after the ceremony, and it was only her indomitable will that kept her going and conscious.

Although Evita was never told the exact nature of her illness, she knew that she was dying and drew up her will leaving her jewellery and other possessions to the people. Her last days were spent with her mother, brother, sisters and Perón by her bedside. More specialists were flown in to see her and when they said there was nothing that could be done for her, Perón told Father Benítez to 'prepare the people' for her death.

On the morning of 26 July, Evita slipped into a coma and Father Benítez administered the last rites. At 8.25 p.m., Eva

Perón died. She was 33. A brief message was broadcast on all radio stations every five minutes that 'At 8:25 p.m., Eva Perón entered immortality'. The whole nation immediately went into deep mourning – films and plays stopped, restaurants and bars closed and within a few minutes of the announcement the whole of Buenos Aires was dark.

Dr Pedro Ara, Professor of Anatomy and embalmer, was on call at the Residence and immediately set to work to prepare Evita's body for public viewing. It was placed in a cedar coffin with a rosary between the fingers and covered with the Argentine flag. The upper portion of the coffin was covered with glass so that her face was visible.

Although preparations had been made for an extended period of national mourning, they did not come close to accommodating the grief of the people. The streets were lined from the Residence to the Ministry of Labour, and as Evita's body was taken to the Ministry, eight people were killed in the crush. Wreaths of flowers filled government buildings and were deposited all over the city under posters of Evita. Within a day of her death there were no flowers left in any flower shop in Argentina. Three days had been set aside for the public to pay their respects, but it was soon evident that this was nowhere near enough. The ceremony was extended for 13 more days and people continued to come from all over the country. Although there was no slackening of public interest the body was

Flowers massed in the street during the lying in state

beginning to dehydrate and the coffin was sealed on 9 August. The coffin was placed on a six-foot-high gun-carriage and carried to Congress by 35 union members. Evita was given the honours of a head of state and the public was allowed to file by again. This was followed by a torch procession outside which ended with hundreds of thousands of torches being simultaneously extinguished at 8.25 p.m. The next day, to Chopin's Funeral March, the *descamisados* pulled the gun-carriage to the union headquarters that Evita had built. The procession included nurses of the Foundation, union members, soldiers, government officials, Perón and Evita's family. The enormous crowd wept and threw flowers.

For the next year, Dr. Ara worked on the embalming of the body so that it would last at least a thousand years. The corpse was filled with solidifying substances and coated with a thin, hard layer of transparent plastic so that it could be displayed and touched and stand up to indefinite contact with the air. As her tomb had yet to be built, a funeral chapel of sorts was set up in the union headquarters where the body was displayed.

Evita, her presence and her absence, deeply affected the Argentine people. Within a month of her death a number of groups put her name forward for canonization, and although not seriously considered by the Vatican, it serves to illustrate just how powerful an impression she made on the people she helped. Streets, subways, and even cities were renamed in her honour and the time of the evening news broadcast was changed from 8.30 p.m. to 8.25 p.m., to commemorate the time of her 'passing into immortality'. Torchlit processions took place on the 22nd of each month and schoolbooks included a prayer to Evita.

Immediately after her death, Perón took her place in the Foundation and the Women's Party, but soon did not have the time or the heart to take on her projects. The leadership positions had to be delegated to others who lacked the charisma and commitment of their founder and the projects floundered. Perón's grief was intense and public and on a number of occasions he seemed lost without her.

As Perón often seemed to have lost his way, so too had his Government. The economic crisis became more severe, corruption was rampant and his security forces began to employ torture as a matter of course. As opposition increased, he legalized divorce and prostitution, which turned the Catholic Church against him and he was excommunicated by the Vatican. Tensions increased with bombing attacks by the navy against Perón, and instead of plunging the country into civil war, on 20 September 1955 Perón boarded a boat and went into exile.

THE CULT OF EVITA

The new military government was in a quandary about what to do with the body of Evita. They were terrified of its power as a rallying symbol for the Perónists, but were equally wary of destroying it and incurring the wrath of the Catholic Church. It was taken off view and placed in a coffin and in essence made to disappear while they decided what to do. Many meetings were held to discuss the 'problem

that Evita the whore, Evita the power-hungry man-eater, Evita the embezzler with a Swiss bank account, etc. came.

This Government-sponsored crucifixion of Evita and purge of Perónism provoked a powerful grassroots response which came to be known as the Resistance. There were many strikes and acts of sabotage which the Government responded to in an even more violent and repressive manner than the Government it had replaced. Thousands of Perónists were arrested and a large number of their leaders executed by firing squad. In this hostile atmosphere, the cult of Evita grew ever stronger and the Perónist years came to be seen as a golden age. Perón, from exile in Spain, fanned the flames of Perónist nostalgia.

By the 1960s a renewed interest in the ideals of Perónism had taken hold of a public disillusioned with long-term military rule, and the character of Evita took a central role. Perónist guerrilla groups sprung up, and one, the Montoneros captured General Aramburu, the former President, in May 1970. The guerrillas questioned him about a number of things, including the whereabouts of Evita's body, which not only was he unwilling, but unable to reveal much. He was shot and a statement was made that his body would not be released to his family until 'the day the remains of our dear comrade Evita are returned to the people'.

When Aramburu's body was discovered, his lawyer passed the letter on to the current President, General Lanusse. President Lanusse was committed to withdrawing the army from the Government and allowing Perónists back in, and saw the 'question of the cadaver' as one that had to be resolved before relationships could be normalized. The letter contained only the name of a cemetery in Milan and that of a priest, who had since died. Military intelligence was sent to Milan to search through the records to find an entry that would fit the circumstances. The record of Maria Maggi de Magistris stated that she was an Italian who had emigrated to Argentina and her body had been returned for burial in 1956, five years after her death. The body was exhumed and driven to Spain in a van, with special diplomatic dispensation to avoid customs.

Isabel Perón

The body was taken to the home of Perón and his new wife, Isabel, in a Madrid suburb. Dr Ara, who was retired and living in Madrid, was called to the Peróns' and escorted to the coffin. He examined the corpse and discovered only minor damage to the outer layer of plastic encasing it. Isabel took care of the corpse, cleaning it up and redoing the hair.

Back in Argentina, terrorist attacks continued while Lanusse tried to figure a way out. In the elections of 1972, Héctor Cámpora stood on Perón's behalf, receiving 49 per cent of the vote. Perón's military rank was restored and Cámpora was allowed to resign to make room for the return of Perón. Perón triumphantly returned to Argentina in November 1973

The embalmed body of Evita lying beside her husband's coffin, 1974

with his third wife, Isabel, but without Evita.

In 1973, Isabel received what had been denied Evita, the vice-presidential candidacy. The Perón-Perón ticket brought Perón his largest majority ever. Perón died in office on 1 July 1974 and Isabel succeeded him. He had not yet fulfilled his promise to bring Evita's body back to Argentina.

The Montoneros again took matters into their own hands. They re-kidnapped Aramburu's body from its family vault to hold hostage until finally, on 17 November 1974, the body of Evita was flown home. The monument planned by the Government of Isabel Perón for Perón and Evita was still in the planning stages, and the bodies were displayed to the faithful in the Presidential Palace. Again, before a memorial could be built the Government was overthrown by a military coup. The new President was unwilling to move into the Presidential Palace with the bodies of Perón and Evita in residence, and so, after 24 years, Evita's body was finally given to her family on 22 October 1976.

The body of Evita now rests in the family vault in the Recoleta Cemetery in Buenos Aires, reserved for prominent, wealthy Argentines. The tomb has a trapdoor which leads to a room housing two coffins with another trapdoor leading to yet another lower level. In this lowest compartment lies Evita's body, buried amongst the Oligarchy she detested, and kept away from the people she loved. The installation was paid for by the Government and the only key to the locked room given to Evita's sister, a final testament to the power, real or imagined, of her lasting influence in the hearts of the *descamisados*.

FURTHER MINI SERIES
INCLUDE

ILLUSTRATED POETS

Robert Burns
Shakespeare
Oscar Wilde
Emily Dickinson
Christina Rossetti
Shakespeare's Love Sonnets

FURTHER MINI SERIES INCLUDE

THEY DIED TOO YOUNG

Elvis
James Dean
Buddy Holly
Jimi Hendrix
Sid Vicious
Marc Bolan
Ayrton Senna
Marilyn Monroe
Jim Morrison

THEY DIED TOO YOUNG

Malcolm X
Kurt Cobain
River Phoenix
John Lennon
Glenn Miller
Isadora Duncan
Rudolph Valentino
Freddie Mercury
Bob Marley

FURTHER MINI SERIES
INCLUDE

HEROES OF THE WILD WEST

General Custer
Butch Cassidy and the Sundance Kid
Billy the Kid
Annie Oakley
Buffalo Bill
Geronimo
Wyatt Earp
Doc Holliday
Sitting Bull
Jesse James